Bulletproof Your Copywriting

12 Sales Copy Legal Dangers And How To Avoid Them

A Quick Legal Guide

By Mike Young, Esq.

Copyright Notice

Table of Contents

How To Use This Guide

Each Quick Legal Guide™ is designed for you to quickly learn the most important things you need to know about one business legal topic.

Whether you're an amateur or professional copywriter, we recommend you read through the Guide from start to finish one time.

Then keep the Guide handy and use it as a reference tool when crafting sales copy for yourself or clients.

For additional help, check out the *Resources* section at MikeYoungLaw.com.

Introduction

"They Laughed When I Said To Obey Copywriting Laws - But When They Got Sued!"[1]

This guide focuses on complying with U.S. federal and state laws. However, many countries have similar laws.

When in doubt about legality, your copywriting should err on the side of caution. For example, don't assume sales copy that's legal in the United States will also be legal to use in the United Kingdom. This also applies to marketing tactics using such copy (e.g., email marketing).

Although copywriting is traditionally known as "salesmanship in *print*,"[2] there are laws and regulations that cover both online marketing (e.g., commercial emails, video sales letters, website sales page, etc.) in addition to offline (e.g., direct response letter sent by postal mail, advertorial in a print magazine, etc.).

To kick things off, let's cover legal and illegal ways to use swipe files.

---

[1] Hat tip to John Caples' ad for music lessons

[2] The late John E. Kennedy is credited with describing copywriting this way.

Chapter 1 - Swipe Files & Fair Use

"Good artists borrow, great artists steal."
- Pablo Picasso

Although it's common to build "swipe" files of successful sales copy written by other copywriting professionals, too often these swipes are illegally misused. Unless you're the Picasso of copywriting, don't expect to get away with stealing over the long term.

Because modern sales copy is rarely in the public domain. Instead, someone owns the copyright to it. This is often the copywriter or the copywriter's client.

Without permission, borrowing and "repurposing" sales copy owned by someone else is intellectual property theft, specifically copyright infringement. Even if you found it on a "swipe" website, chances are it is pirated material.

If you plan to use another copywriter's work, confirm it's in the public domain or get written permission from the person or entity that owns the copyright. Permission may involve payment of a licensing fee.

Now many copywriters do use swipe files legally. How? To research markets they're writing for (e.g., pain points) and to generate ideas on how to sell to those markets using their own words. Because copyright law doesn't protect ideas, it protects how the ideas are expressed.

What about recycling parts of a piece of copy instead of the whole thing? Some copywriters do it (legally or illegally) by claiming "fair use."

What the heck is fair use?

The concept of "fair use" is the ability to use part of a copyrighted work[3] *without* the permission of the copyright owner under certain circumstances.

Unfortunately, fair use is a fact-intensive issue that's resolved on a case-by-case basis. In other words, there's no bright line rule for what is or isn't fair use.

However, there are guidelines courts use you can also apply to your unique situation to help you decide whether you're dealing with fair use or copyright infringement.

Something New

As a preliminary matter, fair use involves something new, i.e., value-added.[4] Cloning parts of someone else's sales copy isn't value-added.

Purpose

Fair use can involve one or one or more of the following purposes: criticism; commentary; parody; reporting news; research; scholarship; and teaching.

This means that if you want to use part of someone else's copyrighted work (or someone wants to use parts of yours

---

[3] Whether or not the copyrighted work is registered.

[4] The concept of adding something new that's value-added is sometimes referred to as "transformative."

without permission), it should be for one or more of these purposes.

Character of Use

Whether the use is commercial (e.g., marketing a product or service) or non-commercial (e.g. non-profit educational) is *a* factor.

Commercial use is *less likely* to be considered fair use. This is typically where a copywriter screws up by repurposing someone else's sales copy without permission. Swapping out company brands in a sales letter to sell a competing product or service isn't fair use.

Nature of the Work

Use of a factual work (e.g., excerpt from a news story) is more likely to be considered fair use than use of a fictional work (e.g., a novel).

Quantity and Quality Used

Generally, the *more* you use of a work, the *less* likely it is considered fair use.

On the other hand, if you use a small portion of a work that's highly valuable (e.g., the paragraph at the end of a mystery novel that reveals the identity of the killer), that's unlikely to be considered fair use.

Note that your view of what's the right amount may differ from what the copyright owner believes.

For example, the Associated Press (AP) once took the position that fair use was limited to four words from any of its news stories (including the headlines).

Effect on Market

If the use negatively affects the market for the copyrighted work, it's less likely to be considered fair use.

For example, "borrowing" parts of someone else's sales copy to sell a competing product would likely have a negative effect on sales of the original product for which the copy was written.

Portraying in a False Light

Caution - Even if use of another's copyrighted work is considered fair use, you can't twist it in your sales copy to portray him in a *false* light that damages his reputation.

For example, don't excerpt a competitor's direct response ad out of context to *falsely* portray the competitor as dishonest, unqualified, etc.

What if you receive a competitor's marketing email filled with grammatical, typographical errors, and a broken hyperlink on the call to action? To the extent fair use applies to quoting some of mistakes, you still can't *falsely* portray the competitor as mentally retarded, functionally illiterate, a tech neanderthal, etc.

When You Can't Rely Upon Fair Use

If you'd like to use someone else's copyrighted work in your sales copy but fair use doesn't apply, what do you do?

Getting permission (preferably in writing) from the copyright owner is the ideal solution. Sometimes permission is given in advance without asking for it (e.g. an affiliate program operator providing template promo emails for affiliates to use).

However, obtaining permission might not be possible if there's no way to identify the copyright owner or if the material you'd like to use is a troll's email, an anonymous review trashing your product, etc, the copywriter is retired/deceased, or the company that originally ran the copy is no longer in business.

In these types of situations, it's important to remember that copyright law doesn't protect ideas, just the way they're expressed.

In your own words,[5] you can describe the idea you're trying to convey. In some cases, it's a hybrid situation, i.e., you take a brief quote (e.g. a phrase or sentence) from the copyrighted work as fair use if it qualifies...and then describe the rest in your own words.

---

[5] Using an article spinner or a thesaurus to simply find-and-replace words isn't enough. That would create a derivative work still covered by the original copyright.

Chapter 2 - Copy Ownership

"No one can come and claim ownership of my work. I am the creator of it, and it lives within me."

- Prince

Sales copy ownership is often mishandled by both copywriter and client. This is true whether the copy is written on an employment or independent contractor basis.

Many clients believe they own the sales copy simply because they paid the copywriter to create it.

On the flip side of the coin, copywriters often believe they have the right to recycle parts of the copy for other clients, particularly in noncompetitive niches.

So, which view is correct? It depends.

If there's not a valid written contract between the parties, chances are no one really knows. And the client's views *will* be different from the copywriter's position on the issue. That's a recipe for disaster.

To avoid this mess, have a written contract that identifies each party's intellectual property rights to the sales copy. This is true whether using an employment agreement or a freelance (independent contractor) copywriting agreement.

Note that there's no single "right" answer to who owns what. So it's a negotiable point based upon what you as the copywriter and the client are both trying to achieve.

Here are some popular solutions.

1. *Active Use Exclusive License*. The copywriter retains ownership of the copy but licenses it to the client for exclusive use until the client stops running the copy. At that point, the copywriter can recycle the copy for other clients.

2. *Active Use Partially Exclusive License*. The copywriter retains ownership of the copy but licenses it to the client for partially exclusive use until the client stops running the copy. For as long as the client runs the copy, the copywriter cannot reuse the copy with others in the client's niche. However, the copywriter can recycle the copy at any time with clients who do not compete with the client.

3. *Time-Limited Exclusive License*. The copywriter retains ownership of the copy but licenses it to the client for exclusive use for a specific time period (e.g., 24 months). At that point, the copywriter can recycle the copy for other clients.

4. *Time-Limited Partially Exclusive License*. The copywriter retains ownership of the copy but licenses it to the client for exclusive use in the client's niche for a specific time period (e.g., 24 months). However, the copywriter can recycle the copy at any time with clients who do not compete with the client. And after the time period has lapsed, the copywriter can use the sales copy with one or more of the client's competitors too.

5. *Client Ownership*. The client pays a premium (e.g., 3x the copywriter's standard rate) in order to own the copyright for the sale copy as work-for-hire. The copywriter has no rights to the copy.

6. *Client Ownership With License To Copywriter*. The client pays a premium (e.g., 2x the copywriter's standard rate) in order to own the copyright for the sales copy as work-for-hire. However, the client grants the copywriter a limited license to reuse the copy with others who do not compete with the client.

7. *Client Ownership With Contingent Copyright Reversion*. The client pays a premium (e.g., 2x the copywriter's standard rate) in order to own the copyright for the sales copy as work-for-hire. However, if (when) the client stops using the copy, the client will transfer copyright ownership back to the copywriter.

Chapter 3 - B2B v. B2C

"Many people want the government to protect the consumer.
A much more urgent problem is to protect the consumer from
the government."
- Milton Friedman

What's one of the easiest ways to reduce legal dangers in sales copy? Where feasible, target businesses (B2B) instead of consumers (B2C) as prospective customers.

Why?

In the United States and other jurisdictions, there are more laws and regulations (and government agencies) protecting consumers than businesses in commercial transactions.

Government agencies consider business owners to be more sophisticated in commercial transactions, i.e. a company assumes the risk when a B2B purchase is made.

However, the same agencies (and the media) presume the business selling a product or service takes advantage of the individual consumer. Think the elderly, single parents, the unemployed, etc. Each is assumed to be a victim in a commercial dispute until proven otherwise.

That's why the typical violation of consumer protection laws permits one or more of the following remedies:

- collection of statutory damages (e.g., triple damages);
- government fines;
- mandatory refunds
- award of attorneys' fees to the "victims;" and

- court costs.

In the United States, consumer protection law violations can lead to action both at the federal level (e.g., the Federal Trade Commission) and one or more of consumer protection agencies of the 50 states. Plus civil lawsuits by plaintiffs' lawyers.

Yes, it's common for copywriting gurus to emphasize writing for one individual as if it were a 1:1 conversation with the prospect. Yet that doesn't preclude making it clear throughout your sales copy that you're making a B2B offer (e.g., "Attention Small Business Owners...") instead of targeting individual consumers.

What if the offer covers both business and consumer prospects? It's a risk judgment call but the safer route is to craft the copy targeting the business prospects while letting consumers also purchase if they want to.

If nothing else, it provides you (and your client) a stronger defense against any alleged violation of consumer rights. And the sales copy is less likely to be on the radar of a government agency for scrutiny if B2B in nature.

What if the offer can't be crafted as B2B? In other words, what if you're writing sales copy primarily for a consumer market? The next chapters (*Material Connections Disclosures* and *False & Deceptive Claims*) are particularly important for reducing risks when selling to consumers.

Chapter 4 - Material Connections Disclosures

"Seldom, very seldom, does complete truth belong to any human disclosure; seldom can it happen that something is not a little disguised, or a little mistaken." - Jane Austen

Material connections are key relationships that must be disclosed in your sales copy so that the recipients can make an informed decision about purchasing the product or service you're promoting.

Affiliate Status

The most common material connection is promotion as an affiliate in exchange for a commission.

There isn't specific language required for disclosing affiliate status.[6] You can use your own words to disclose this type of material connection. Here's an example for a copywriting product I promote as an affiliate.

"Because Scott Haines' 'Shortcut Copywriting Secrets' is such a great course for both new and experienced copywriters, it's one of the few resources I recommend as an affiliate. This means if you get the course through this link, I may be compensated."

---

[6] And you don't have to disclose how much you'll get paid as an affiliate either. Just affiliate status.

Don't hide the disclosure in small print. It's good practice to use a text font size and color matching the main body's text.

Avoid using a text color that matches the background color so no one can read it (e.g., white text on a white background). That's not disclosure. It's deceptive.

Other Common Material Connections

Naturally, there are other material connections that are essential facts you should disclose in copy that markets to consumers. They include...

- You are related to (or dating) the person whose product or service you're promoting.
- You're promoting someone else's product or service to your list in exchange for them promoting your product or service to their list
- A seminar promoter has agreed to let you speak at an event if you pitch the seminar to your lists.
- You'll receive a free membership site subscription if you sell X number of memberships to that site.
- You received a free/complimentary/review copy of a product or service in exchange for promoting the product or service (including providing a review).

Chapter 5 - False And Deceptive Claims

"You are never so easily fooled as when trying to fool someone else." - François de La Rochefoucauld

Whether it's your sales copy, or a testimonial you include in a marketing email, it's important to make sure your health and money-related claims for the products and services you're promoting comply with the law.

What The Wrong Claims Can Cost A Business

The U.S. Federal Trade Commission (FTC), a state's Attorney General, or another government agency[7] can destroy a business for making the wrong claims when marketing to consumers. We're talking fines, mandatory refunds of all purchases, triple damages, asset freezes, and restrictions or a ban on future marketing.[8]

---

[7] e.g., U.S. Food & Drug Administration (FDA)

[8] A client rejected an affiliate applicant because he had received two permanent bans by the FTC...one for online marketing and a second for offline marketing. Although the applicant lied on his application, a simple Google search of the applicant's name and FTC revealed the bans.

And even if a business "wins" when the government comes after it, the legal fees will likely wipe out any profits generated by making the claims.

Of course, there are also consumer protection attorneys who will sue on behalf of the "victims" if there's money to be made. Plus many consumer protection laws[9] make a business pay the consumer's attorney's fees and court costs when the business loses the lawsuit.

Atypical Results Disclaimers

Now some copywriters mistakenly believe they can make earnings or health claims if they include an atypical results disclaimer somewhere in their sales copy.

Example: If you buy the *Crypto Real Estate Billionaire Course*, you could earn $47,000 per month like Jessica Smith did. Of course, your results might be different.

Example Testimonial Claim: "I lost 65 lbs. in only 30 days by drinking Magic Protein Shakes." - John Jones, Hot Springs, Arkansas. Your results may vary but we promise you'll shed weight like John by replacing two of your meals daily with our delicious shakes.

---

[9] Some copywriters focus on writing for business-to-business (B2B) markets instead of business-to-consumer (B2C) to reduce the risk of getting in trouble under consumer protection laws.

Although these disclaimers *might* help you avoid liability in some states, the FTC doesn't believe such disclaimers are enough.

What Are Typical Results?

Using the second example, let's say you have 100,000 customers buying Magic Protein Shakes. And 250 of them have provided testimonials backed by proof (pics, medical records, etc.) showing they averaged 90 lbs. of weight loss over six months while drinking the shakes.

While these testimonials may be anecdotal evidence the protein shakes work, making a related weight loss claim would be considered deceptive.

Why?

Because the FTC and some other government agencies assume the other 99,750 customers who didn't provide testimonials either lost no weight or even gained weight while drinking the shakes.

How To Make Claims The Right Way

Here are two simple solutions:

1. Scientific studies; and
2. Customer case studies backed by evidence

Scientific Studies

Although it's often too expensive to pay for scientific studies to provide you with results you can claim, there may be legitimate third-party studies you can rely upon in your copywriting.

Example: You're writing copy to market a financial newsletter subscription to small business owners. You find a peer-reviewed study in the *Journal of Business and Economic Statistics* that concludes entrepreneurs who read financial newsletters monthly earn an extra $100,000 per year on their investments than those who don't read any financial publications.

You *can* cite the study and its findings in your sales copy.[10]

However, do not make the claim that purchasing the financial newsletter will result in the subscriber achieving similar results. The reader of your sales copy *may* reach that conclusion but you don't have a study showing the newsletter's subscribers actually earn $100,000 more per year.

And don't claim or imply that either the authors of the study or the *Journal's* publisher have endorsed the financial newsletter you're promoting either.

Example: You market minimalist running shoes to retirees by mail. You discover a peer-reviewed study in *The Lancet* that concludes men over 65 who run 30 minutes three times

---

[10] You cannot falsely state or imply that the publication has endorsed the product or service you're marketing.

weekly lose an average of 2.5 pounds monthly and decrease their chance of a heart attack or stroke by 17%.

In your sales, you *can* cite the study and its findings. However, do <u>not</u> claim that wearing running shoes will cause the purchaser to achieve these results. Instead, let the prospects make the mental leap by themselves that investing in these shoes results in similar health benefits.

And don't state or imply that the study's authors or *The Lancet* have endorsed the minimalist running shoes either.

Customer Case Studies

In your sales copy, you *can* refer and link to legitimate[11] customer case studies to support your claims. Although this guide is not about writing case studies, a good format is to identify (a) the prospect's problem, (b) your product/service as the solution, and (c) the results[12] achieved with your solution.

The case studies you link to should include all of the material facts that led to the results.

Example: A customer who lost 90 lbs. by drinking your client's protein shakes also worked out two hours daily at the gym and was on a 1500-calorie diet. Both the daily exercise and the diet

---

[11] Never create fake case studies or testimonials. They're deceptive and there's no defense if you get caught.

[12] Don't use stale testimonials or case studies. At least on an annual basis, make sure they're still accurate as far as results. Update or dump them if they're inaccurate.

should be disclosed in the case study because they are material facts.

Keep Good Records

Keep copies of scientific studies and the supporting documentation you have for claims made in case studies. If a government agency investigates, having these records to back up what you wrote in your sales copy reduces the likelihood of a formal government investigation or an expensive lawsuit.

Chapter 6 - Trashing The Competition

"You're only as smart as your dumbest competitor." - Gordon Bethune

General Rule

It's okay to refer to the competition in sales copy so long as what's being said isn't false or misleading. In the United States, truth is a defense to defamation claims.

However, note that isn't the case in all jurisdictions (e.g., the United Kingdom).

So be careful when emphasizing the negative aspects of a competitor's products or services instead of focusing on the positive aspects of the one you're promoting.

Accurate feature comparisons and related benefits are fairly safe to use.

Example: "Widget X only does A. However, our new Gizmo Y does A, B, and C, which means you'll..."

It's also good to use *reputable* studies showing preference for what your product or service offers.

Of course, if you or your client paid for the study being cited, that should be disclosed as a material fact too. Naturally, for a study to be "reputable" it should be scientific.

For instance, asking 3 people their opinion of competing products isn't a statistically valid sample. And that 2 of the 3 preferred your client's product over the competitor's doesn't mean you can assert that 66% of the market prefers your client's product.

Competing Brands

What about your competitor's brands?

You can typically refer to your competitor's trademarks or service marks if you (1) don't cause confusion (dilute the brand) in the marketplace and (2) make it clear you're not claiming ownership of the marks.

For example, comparing your client's Brand X to a competitor's Brand Y is generally acceptable if you're not misrepresenting the features and benefits of Brand Y.

However, sales copy written to make the reader think they're buying competitor's Brand Y but the call to action drives them to purchase your client's Brand X would be considered deceptive and dilutes the value of the competitor's mark by causing confusion in the marketplace.

Chapter 7 - Copyright Notice & Registration

"Education is when you read the fine print. Experience is what you get when you don't." - Pete Seeger

Copyright Notice

To reduce the chance someone will pirate your sales copy, you'll want to put a copyright notice on it. For website content, you can put the notice in the site's footer. For marketing emails, place below your signature lines at the end of each message.

Example:

Copyright © 2023 Law Office of Michael E. Young PLLC.[13] All rights reserved. Unauthorized duplication prohibited.

This notice is enough to prevent someone from claiming they didn't know about your copyright ownership.

However, the notice is only of limited value for protecting your sales copy unless you also register your copyright.

---

[13] Hyperlinking to your website in the copyright notice is optional.

Copyright Registration

To put some legal teeth behind your copyright, consider copyright registration.[14] In the United States, that's done with the U.S. Copyright Office at the Library of Congress.

You can file online at Copyright.gov. To save money, some copywriters register multiple works as a single compilation.

For example, one can bundle an email marketing campaign (series of emails) together and register them for a single filing fee instead of separate registrations (and fees) for each separate email.

What's the advantage of copyright registration? It gives you a legal sledgehammer to hit pirates who swipe your sales copy.

Why? Because willful infringers can be liable for up to $150,000 per infringement, attorneys' fees, and court costs.

---

[14] Note that some countries do not have a copyright registration system.

Chapter 8 - Advertorial Disclosures

"We can't have, like, willy-nilly proliferation of fake news. That's crazy." - Elon Musk

Although it will depend in part on where published, advertorials often require a disclosure (e.g., "ADVERTISEMENT" at the top). This is so that readers know the copy isn't an objective editorial or news article in order to make an informed decision before taking action based on the copy.

Even where such a requirement isn't imposed by the law or the publication running the advertorial, it's still a good idea to weave the disclosure into the sales copy when targeting consumer markets.

For example, a business relationship (e.g., affiliate status, joint venture, etc.) can be revealed by using phrases like "We've teamed up with," "we've partnered with," etc.

Chapter 9 - Pseudonyms & Celebrity Endorsements

"The man creates a pseudonym and hides behind it like a worm." - Sylvia Plath

Pseudonyms

Generally, using pseudonyms in sales copy is permissible. However, there are important exceptions to this rule.

For instance, you should not adopt a pen name that impersonates someone else.

Example: You write an ad that sells youth summer basketball camps and adopt the pen name "LeBron James." That's a recipe for getting sued by NBA professional basketball player Lebron James.

Or you write copy signed with the pseudonym *"K.J. Rowling"* to sell guided "magical English and Scottish castle tours." The public would mistakenly assume by your pen name that the copy was written by *J.K.* Rowling, author of the Harry Potter book series.

In short, pseudonyms are fine in copywriting if not used for fraudulent or deceptive purposes.

Do some research on a potential pen name before using it to ensure there won't be a likelihood of confusion in the market between your pseudonym and someone with that name or something very similar.

Celebrity Endorsements

What if you want to use a famous name in your sales copy to add third-party credibility?

The safest way to do this is to get written authorization from that person, which typically involves compensation for the endorsement.

Some copywriters try to evade the compensation part by quoting a famous person in the copy on the assumption that readers will believe the person has endorsed the product or service.

However, if the copy is written to create such a mistaken assumption, don't be surprised if that celebrity's lawyers reach out with a cease-and-desist demand at a minimum.

Remember that a celebrity's endorsement has value. And most want to be compensated for giving it.

Note that in many jurisdictions you will have to clearly disclose the fact that the celebrity was compensated for their endorsement (See *Chapter 4 - Material Connections Disclosures*). So the prospective purchasers can evaluate the value of that endorsement in light of the compensation received.

Chapter 10 - Sales Copy Signatures

"What an author likes to write most is his signature on the back of a cheque." - Brendan Behan

If a business structure has a personal liability shield (e.g., a corporation or limited liability company (LLC)), take advantage of that shield by signing the sales copy correctly (e.g., a direct response marketing sales letter or email).

How do you do this?

The three essential elements of a proper signature are:

1. Identify the signer by name;
2. State the signatory's company title; and
3. Include the full name of the business

Example signature:

Sincerely,

-Heyward

Heyward Skultz, President
Skarbux Coffee & Tea, Inc.

There's risk of personal liability exposure by the signer if it isn't clear the sales copy is being sent on behalf of the business.

In the above example, if Heyward signed just his name without identifying his title or company name, people could assume he was sending it in his individual capacity instead of for the business.

What about using a pseudonym? This is permissible if not fraudulent or misleading (*See Chapter 9 - Pseudonyms & Celebrity Endorsements*).

For example, sometimes there will be a name switch to match target market demographics (e.g., gender, age, ethnicity, etc.).

However, even a pen name should sign on behalf of the business entity to take advantage of the personal liability shield.

Chapter 11 - Entity Liability Shield

"Corporation: an ingenious device for obtaining profit without individual responsibility." - Ambrose Bierce

In the United States, there are four common ways to set up your copywriting business:

(1) Sole Proprietorship;

(2) General Partnership;

(3) Subchapter "S" Corporation; and

(4) Limited Liability Company

The first two choices can be fatal even if you have an excellent business plan and the skills to implement it.

Here's why...

Sole Proprietorships Stink

A sole proprietorship means you own the assets and liabilities of your copywriting business personally. You get all of the benefits of the money coming in but also are personally on the hook when things go wrong. There's no liability shield in place.

If your copywriting business is sued, this means you're sued. Even if your sole proprietorship is doing business under a fictitious name (a.k.a. assumed name or doing-business-as) you've registered with the government, you're still on the hook personally to pay if you lose in court.

In some states, a plaintiff who successfully sues you and gets a judgment can go after your house, your bank accounts, your car, and other personal assets to get paid.

General Partnerships Can Hurt You Too

Do you want to know what's worse than a sole proprietorship for owning a copywriting business? A general partnership.

Although there are several types of partnerships, most partnerships are *general* partnerships. This type of partnership typically occurs when two or more people share equally in the assets and liabilities of the business.

Like a sole proprietorship, you get all of the potential personal liability plus more legal grenades thrown your way from time to time.

A general partnership is like a marriage...only more so. When it falls apart, expect the "divorce from Hell." This can include lawsuits between partners, money taken, assets sold, and a host of other problems. If one partner gets into financial difficulties, the partnership's assets can disappear quickly before another partner will discover what's happening.

And it gets worse...

In many cases, your partner (and employees) can create personal liabilities for you. You may be held responsible for the contracts signed by your partner, partnership debts incurred by your partner, and even for the personal injuries caused when your partner's kid has a car wreck on the way to get office supplies for your business.

And what happens if your partner's marriage or personal finances are on the rocks? Do you want to watch your partnership's assets fought over in a divorce court or in personal bankruptcy proceedings?

Like a sole proprietorship, business insurance (see the next chapter) is a good idea for a general partnership. Yet it may not protect you from many common partnership liabilities.

Most professional copywriters recognize the risks of sole proprietorships and general partnerships are too great for long-term success.

Limiting Partnership Liability

In addition to general partnerships, some jurisdictions have variations for limiting partner liability for the business and acts of other partners. These types of partnerships are known by names such as "Limited Partnerships," "Limited Liability Partnerships," etc. The rights and responsibilities of the partners are typically determined by the law of the jurisdiction where they are formed.

That being said, few professional U.S.-based copywriters choose these types of partnerships because there are alternative entities (Subchapter S corporations and limited liability companies) that are more attractive for tax reduction, simplicity, and liability shield purposes.

Subchapter S Corporations

Some U.S. professional copywriters use Subchapter S corporations. "Subchapter S" refers to a section of the U.S. Internal Revenue Code giving special tax benefits to this type of corporation. When you hear a small business owner tell you he owns a corporation, most of the time this means he owns the shares of a Subchapter S corporation.

Many large publicly traded companies are organized as Subchapter C corporations. A Subchapter C corporation has its income taxed twice, once at the corporate level and a second time on the capital gains passed on to its shareholders.

In contrast, a Subchapter S corporation is taxed once on its income at the shareholder level for capital gains. If the corporation qualifies for Subchapter S status at both the federal and state level, a copywriter can see major tax savings by having avoided the double taxation imposed on a Subchapter C corporation instead. Rarely does it make sense to set up a copywriting business as a C corporation.

Of course, this is something you should discuss with your accountant before deciding based on taxes to be paid.

Entity Liability Shields

The Subchapter S corporation also offers (and so does a Subchapter C corporation) a personal liability shield to protect you in ways unavailable for a general partnership or a sole proprietorship. Under the law, the corporation is considered an entity separate from you. A fictitious person, the corporation can own assets and incur liabilities for which you are not personally liable.

When you play by the rules and observe business formalities, the entity liability shield should protect your personal assets if the business gets sued or the government launches an investigation.

Combined with business insurance, a Subchapter S corporation creates a certain peace of mind because it is unlikely your personal assets will be touched.

Now before you decide to form a Subchapter S corporation for your copywriting business, consider what a limited liability company has to offer.

Limited Liability Companies

Until the mid-1990s, limited liability companies (LLCs) were uncommon in the United States although they have existed for many years in Europe. States started passing laws enabling limited liability companies to be formed here.

When used correctly, LLCs have most of the same advantages as Subchapter S corporations both for income taxation and as a shield from personal liability.

One of the major advantages of a limited liability company over a Subchapter S corporation is how easy it is to run it. An LLC operating agreement can be very flexible for its members (owners) to use when compared to the formalities shareholders (owners), officers, and directors have for running a corporation.

If you don't like the thought of corporate resolutions, board of directors' meetings, shareholders meetings, and other such activities, you should seriously consider an LLC.

Please note, however, in some states an LLC may be taxed differently than a Subchapter S corporation and may have different protections. An LLC may also have different federal tax issues.

Because the IRS gives you the flexibility to choose how you want the LLC treated for tax purposes. In some cases, you may want to elect to have your LLC taxed as if it were a Subchapter S corporation. In other circumstances, it may make sense to have your LLC taxed as if it were a sole proprietorship or a partnership.

Note that these are options for reducing your tax burden. Electing to have your LLC taxed as a Subchapter S corporation, sole proprietorship, or partnership does *not* affect your entity liability shield. Your conduct determines whether the shield stays in place.

The tax issue is separate and simply the IRS and some states' departments of revenue giving you a choice on how you want to have your LLC's income taxed.

Consult with your business lawyer and accountant before deciding about the best type of business entity and tax election for you.

Business Entity Location

Nearly every "business opportunity" seminar these days has some asset protection or tax guru selling scams involving setting up corporations or limited liability companies. These con artists may be lawyers or accountants, which unfortunately gives them credibility when they lie to you from the stage.

Don't believe the hype. It could cost you your copywriting business - and even put you in prison!

Twenty-five years ago, the same scam was being pitched for other states, such as Maine and Delaware. The only thing different these days is which states are popular (currently New Mexico, Nevada, and Wyoming).

Now the typical con artist selling these scams will tell you his system is unique because it will protect/hide your assets plus you will pay little or no income taxes.

Sounds too good to be true? It is if you get caught.

Unless you actually live and run your business in New Mexico, Nevada, or Wyoming, chances are you've been conned.

Why?

Let's say you live in Texas but set up a Nevada corporation for the tax and asset benefits. You operate your copywriting business from your home in Texas, and even have your Nevada corporation set up a business checking account at your local Texas bank.

Are you really doing business in Nevada or are you actually doing business in Texas?

Where have you qualified to do business?

The State of Nevada will be happy to take your annual fees, but the State of Texas is going to be very interested in the business you're doing too.

In fact, to qualify to do business in most states, you must either set up your business entity there or otherwise register to do business in the state as a foreign entity. In Texas, for example, this would mean registering your Nevada corporation (or LLC) with the Texas Secretary of State's Office.

And this means registration fees, franchise tax filings in Texas, and filing an annual report listing the officers for your Nevada entity with the Texas Secretary of State's Office.

To recap, you're now doing paperwork in both Nevada and Texas, possibly paying taxes in both states, and making a public record in Texas of who controls your business (say goodbye to privacy).

What if you get caught? What the con artist is counting on is the idea you won't get caught.

And you might not...but what if you do?

Let's look at Texas as an example.

"If a foreign entity [such as a Nevada corporation or LLC] transacts business in Texas without registering,

* the entity cannot maintain an action, suit, or proceeding in a Texas court until it registers;

* the attorney general can enjoin (stop) the entity from transacting business in Texas;

* the entity is subject to a civil penalty equal to all fees and taxes that would have been imposed if the entity had registered when first required; and

* if the entity has transacted business in the state for more than ninety (90) days, the Secretary of State will impose a late filing fee for an Application for Registration equal to the registration fee for each year or part of year of delinquency."[15]

There you have it. Back taxes and penalties.

Will the con artist who sold you the Nevada entity be around to pay these? Or will you be stuck?

What about personal liability?

If your corporation or limited liability company hasn't qualified to do business in the state where it actually does business, there's a real danger the entity liability shield will disappear. If your business gets sued, the court could ignore the existence of your corporation or limited liability company, treat it as a sole proprietorship, and you'd be on the hook personally to satisfy any judgment against you or your business.

---

[15] Source: The Texas Secretary of State's website.

And, of course, there's the personal liability for those taxes you didn't pay to the state for those years you didn't register your entity to do business.

Can you use these entities to hide your identity?

Con artists who sell Nevada and Wyoming entities will sometimes do so based on alleged privacy protections. Some will go so far as to make unsubstantiated claims about the ability to use bearer shares and the effect of using such shares. Transfers of bearer shares, by gift or sale, can trigger a taxable event both at the federal and state level.

Even assuming an idea like this is possible, and there are no particular tax consequences when a transfer is made, there's also the matter of identifying who controls the company when you file an annual report with the state where you actually do business.

What good is hiding your identity in State A when the business entity must disclose it in State B?

Won't the laws in the state you formed the business entity protect you? Just because you set up a Nevada entity doesn't mean Nevada law will apply if you get sued in another state.

The law of the state where you're sued, not Nevada's law, is most likely going to determine what will happen to you. If you're sued in federal court, federal rules of civil procedure will govern, and the substantive law will probably be either federal law or the state law in the place where you're sued.

What's this all mean?

If you're really running your copywriting business in the state where you live, don't fall for the slick talking pitch selling you on setting up a corporation or LLC elsewhere for tax or asset protection savings.

Consult with your own experts and make wise decisions as to the type of entity you really need and where it should be formed.

Remember proper tax avoidance (minimizing your taxes) is legal. Tax evasion (not paying taxes you owe) is illegal. The latter can cost you a lot of money and even lead to criminal charges for tax fraud.

Chapter 12 - Liability Insurance

"There are worse things in life than death. Have you ever spent an evening with an insurance salesman?" - Woody Allen

Business liability insurance is great if:

(a) you can afford it;

(b) the policy covers what you're sued for; and

(c) the insurance company decides to defend you in the lawsuit and pay the claim if needed.

Regardless of what type of business entity you choose (e.g., LLC), you should seriously consider getting liability insurance to cover your copywriting business.

However, some insurers decide it makes more sense to deny you coverage when you're sued because chances are you don't have the resources to fight the insurance company's lawyers in court to get coverage under a policy you've paid for.

Not fair? That's life.

The CEO of a very large insurance company bragged about how his company would settle no claim before its time. What he meant is even if a claim was valid, the insurance company wasn't going to pay out unless it absolutely had to.

Although this CEO lost his job shortly thereafter, you have to wonder if it was because of something he did or because he revealed how the insurance game is really played by some of the bad guys in the industry.

Even if you've got the friendliest insurance agent in the world, his job is to collect premiums and the insurance company he represents never wants you to make a claim...just keep paying those premiums.

Yes. As a copywriter, you should carry business liability insurance to meet your needs. In many instances, this will include a general liability policy and an umbrella policy.

However, your insurance company may not come to your rescue. And if you're working as a copywriter without an entity as a liability shield, you can be financially destroyed.

Do You Need Help?

Do you need copywriting legal advice?

Let's talk. Go to

https://mikeyounglaw.com/appointments/

Or call 1-214-546-4247 to schedule your phone consultation.

Just choose a day and time that's convenient and I'll call you.

Regards,

-Mike

Michael E. Young, J.D., LL.M.
Attorney & Counselor at Law

About The Author

Since 1994, Internet Lawyer Mike Young has helped business clients (including many copywriters) prevent and solve legal problems.

President of the Internet Attorneys Association LLC, Mike has a law office in Plano, Texas (a Dallas suburb).

A happily married father with three sons, Mike enjoys spending time with his family, walking his dogs, and self-defense training.

To learn more, go to MikeYoungLaw.com. While there, subscribe to his complimentary newsletter where you will receive important business legal news and tips by email.

And be sure to check out the website's *Resources* section for additional helpful information.

Disclosures And Disclaimers

Neither the Author nor the Publisher makes any claim to the intellectual property rights of third-party vendors, their subsidiaries, or related entities.

All trademarks and service marks are the properties of their respective owners. All references to these properties are made solely for editorial purposes. Except for marks owned by the Author or the Publisher, no commercial claims are made to their use, and neither the Author nor the Publisher is affiliated with such marks in any way.

Unless otherwise expressly noted, none of the individuals or business entities mentioned herein has endorsed the contents of this guide.

Limits of Liability & Disclaimers of Warranties

Because this guide is a general educational information product, it is not a substitute for professional advice on the topics discussed in it.

The materials in this guide are provided "as is" and without warranties of any kind either express or implied. The Author and the Publisher disclaim all warranties, express or implied, including, but not limited to, implied warranties of merchantability and fitness for a particular purpose. The Author and the Publisher do not warrant that defects will be corrected, or that any website or any server that makes this guide available is free of viruses or other harmful components. The Author does not warrant or make any representations regarding the use or the results of the use of the materials in this guide in terms of their correctness, accuracy, reliability, or otherwise. Applicable law may not allow the exclusion of implied warranties, so the above exclusion may not apply to you.

Under no circumstances, including, but not limited to, negligence, shall the Author or the Publisher be liable for any special or consequential damages that result from the use of, or the inability to use this guide, even if the Author, the Publisher, or an authorized representative has been advised of the possibility of such damages.

Applicable law may not allow the limitation or exclusion of liability or incidental or consequential damages, so the above limitation or exclusion may not apply to you. In no event shall the Author's or Publisher's total liability to you for all damages, losses, and causes of action (whether in contract, tort, including but not limited to, negligence or otherwise) exceed the amount paid by you, if any, for this guide.

You agree to hold the Author and the Publisher of this guide, principals, agents, affiliates, and employees harmless from any and all liability for all claims for damages due to injuries, including attorney fees and costs, incurred by you or caused to third parties by you, arising out of the products, services, and activities discussed in this guide, excepting only claims for gross negligence or intentional tort.

You agree that any and all claims for gross negligence or intentional tort shall be settled solely by confidential binding arbitration per the American Arbitration Association's commercial arbitration rules. All arbitration must occur in the municipality where the Author's principal place of business is located. Your claim cannot be aggregated with third party claims. Arbitration fees and costs shall be split equally, and you are solely responsible for your own lawyer fees.

Facts and information are believed to be accurate at the time they were placed in this guide. All data provided in this guide is to be used for information purposes only. The information contained within is not intended to provide specific legal, financial, tax, physical or mental health advice, or any other advice whatsoever, for any individual or company and should not be relied upon in that regard. The services described are only offered in jurisdictions where they may be legally offered. Information provided is not all-inclusive, and is limited to information that is made available and such information should not be relied upon as all-inclusive or accurate.

For more information about this policy, please contact the Author at the e-mail address listed in the Copyright Notice at the front of this guide.

IF YOU DO NOT AGREE WITH THESE TERMS AND EXPRESS CONDITIONS, DO NOT READ THIS GUIDE. YOUR USE OF THIS GUIDE, PRODUCTS, SERVICES, AND ANY PARTICIPATION IN ACTIVITIES MENTIONED IN THIS GUIDE, MEAN THAT YOU ARE AGREEING TO BE LEGALLY BOUND BY THESE TERMS.

Affiliate Compensation & Material Connections Disclosure

This guide may contain hyperlinks to websites and information created and maintained by other individuals and organizations. The Author and the Publisher do not control or guarantee the accuracy, completeness, relevance, or timeliness of any information or privacy policies posted on these linked websites.

You should assume that all references to products and services in this guide are made because material connections exist between the Author or Publisher and the providers of the mentioned products and services ("Provider").

You should also assume that all hyperlinks within this guide are affiliate links for (a) the Author, (b) the Publisher, or (c) someone else who is an affiliate for the mentioned products and services (individually and collectively, the "Affiliate").

The Affiliate recommends products and services in this guide based in part on a good faith belief that the purchase of such products or services will help readers in general.

The Affiliate has this good faith belief because (a) the Affiliate has tried the product or service mentioned prior to recommending it or (b) the Affiliate has researched the reputation of the Provider and has made the decision to recommend the Provider's products or services based on the Provider's history of providing these or other products or services.

The representations made by the Affiliate about products and services reflect the Affiliate's honest opinion based upon the facts known to the Affiliate at the time this guide was published.

Because there is a material connection between the Affiliate and Providers of products or services mentioned in this guide, you should always assume that the Affiliate may be biased because of the Affiliate's relationship with a Provider and/or because the Affiliate has received or will receive something of value from a Provider.

Perform your own due diligence before purchasing a product or service mentioned in this guide.

The type of compensation received by the Affiliate may vary. In some instances, the Affiliate may receive complimentary products (such as a review copy), services, or money from a Provider prior to mentioning the Provider's products or services in this guide.

In addition, the Affiliate may receive a monetary commission or non-monetary compensation when you take action by clicking on a hyperlink in this guide. This includes, but is not limited to, when you purchase a product or service from a Provider after clicking on an affiliate link in this guide.

Purchase Price

Although the Publisher believes the price is fair for the value that you receive, you understand and agree that the purchase price for this guide has been arbitrarily set by the Publisher or the vendor who sold you this guide. This price bears no relationship to objective standards.

Due Diligence

You are advised to do your own due diligence when it comes to making any decisions. Use caution and seek the advice of qualified professionals before acting upon the contents of this guide or any other information. You shall not consider any examples, documents, or other content in this guide or otherwise provided by the Author or Publisher to be the equivalent of professional advice.